Dear Reader,

Discover 55 delicious, super-easy keto casserole recipes th[at...] again

Each recipe is specifically designed to stay within the keto diet guidelines and to satisfy your cravings, and boost your energy levels.

You'll find in this cookbook:

- Scrumptious casseroles for one that are under 6 g net carbs per meal
- Full-color illustrations of every recipe
- Pre-calculated macros and calories for every delicious dish
- Chicken, pork, beef, fish, egg, and vegetable casseroles
- And so much more!

Whether you're just beginning your weight loss journey or you're an experienced keto dieter, this keto-friendly cookbook is the perfect tool to help keep you on track and inspire you to explore new foods and flavors.

Thank you for buying this book!

Wish you a happy and healthy life,
Tibor Szentkiralyi

P.S. If you have any questions just email me at tibor@getelan.com

Table of Content

Chicken Casserole with Brussels Sprouts and Bacon 4

Chicken Ketochilada Casserole 5

Bacon-wrapped Chicken Drumsticks 6

Mustard Chicken Thighs 7

Chicken Breast with Vegetables 8

Sour Chicken Breast with Vegetables 9

Mushroom Chicken Breast 10

Zucchini Chicken Casserole 11

Four Cheese Chicken Casserole 12

Sour Chicken Drumsticks 13

Tomato Chicken Drumsticks 14

Chicken Breast Casserole with Pickles and Bacon 15

Eggplant Chicken Breast Casserole 16

Spinach Chicken Breast Casserole 17

Cottage Pie 18

Mushroom Beef Tenderloin 19

Beef Casserole with Eggplant and Tomato 20

Cabbage Beef Casserole 21

Keto Beef Meatballs 22

Beef Casserole with Vegetables 23

Beef Casserole with Egg 24

Zucchini Beef Casserole 25

Mushroom Beef Casserole 26

Tomato Beef Meatballs 27

Mushroom Pork Casserole 28

Cheese Pork Meatballs 29

Mustard Pork Casserole 30

Tomato Pork Casserole 31

Eggplant Pork Casserole 32

Layered Pork Casserole 33

Bacon Pork Casserole 34

Bell Pepper Pork Casserole 35

Bacon Roast Pork Casserole 36

Zucchini Pork Casserole 37

Pork Stuffed Cabbage 38

Pork Meatballs 39

Cauliflower Salami Casserole	40
Omelet Sausage Casserole	41
Green Bean with Bacon	42
Liver Casserole	43
Kingklip Casserole	44
Salmon Casserole	45
Broccoli Salmon Casserole	46
Tomato Shrimp Casserole	47
Butter Shrimp Casserole	48
Mushroom White Fish Casserole	49
Sour White Fish Casserole	50
Mushroom Egg Casserole	51
Sour Zucchini Casserole	52
Brussels Sprouts Casserole	53
Cabbage Zucchini Casserole	54
Eggplant Zucchini Casserole	55
Tomato Eggplant Casserole	56
Egg Kale Casserole	57
Tomato Mushroom Casserole	58
You're Just One Keto Game Away From	59

Chicken Casserole with Brussels Sprouts and Bacon

Ingredients

3.5 oz (99 g) Chicken breast (boneless)

1.5 oz (43 g) Bacon

3.5 oz (99 g) Brussels sprouts

1.0 oz (28 g) Cheese

0.5 oz (14 g) Mayonnaise (80%)

Salt, pepper, and spices to taste

Energy: 524 kcal

Protein: 38 g

Fat: 37 g

Net Carbs: 6 g

Total Carbs: 10 g

Directions

Preheat oven to 360 °F (180 °C). Lightly grease a casserole with cooking oil.

Cut chicken and bacon into chunks; place in the casserole, then mix with Brussels sprouts, mayonnaise and pepper. Usually, bacon gives enough salt to the meal; if you want it to be more seasoned apply your favorite spices.

Bake it for ~20 min covered or stirring occasionally, then place shredded cheese on top. Bake it for extra ~10 min.

Chicken Ketochilada Casserole

Ingredients

5.0 oz (142 g) Chicken breast (boneless)

3.5 oz (99 g) Avocado

1.0 oz (28 g) Olive

1.0 oz (28 g) Cheddar

1.0 oz (28 g) Enchilada Sauce

Salt, pepper, and spices to taste

Energy: 493 kcal

Protein: 41 g

Fat: 31 g

Net Carbs: 4 g

Total Carbs: 12 g

Directions

Preheat oven to 360 °F (180 °C). Lightly grease a casserole with cooking oil.

Cut chicken and avocado into chunks; place in the casserole, then mix with olives and enchilada sauce.

Bake it for ~20 min covered or stirring occasionally, then place shredded cheese on top. Bake it for extra ~10 min.

Bacon-wrapped Chicken Drumsticks

Ingredients

7.0 oz (199 g) Chicken drumsticks

1.5 oz (43 g) Bacon

1.0 oz (28 g) Olive

3.5 oz (99 g) Tomato

1/4 teaspoon Thyme

Salt, pepper, and spices to taste

Energy: 451 kcal

Protein: 45 g

Fat: 27 g

Net Carbs: 3 g

Total Carbs: 5 g

Directions

Preheat oven to 360 °F (180 °C). Lightly grease a casserole with cooking oil.

Wrap chicken drumsticks in bacon and place in the casserole, then put thyme, olives, and tomatoes on top.

Bake it for ~45 min turning drumsticks over occasionally or covered.

Mustard Chicken Thighs

Ingredients

7.0 oz (199 g) Chicken thighs

2.0 oz (57 g) Bell pepper

0.5 oz (14 g) Mustard

0.5 oz (14 g) Chopped almond

1/4 teaspoon Parsley

Salt, pepper, and spices to taste

Energy: 354 kcal

Protein: 43 g

Fat: 16 g

Net Carbs: 5 g

Total Carbs: 8 g

Directions

Preheat oven to 360 °F (180 °C). Lightly grease a casserole with cooking oil.

Mix chicken thighs with mustard, almond, and bell pepper in the casserole.

Bake it for ~30 min turning meat over occasionally or covered, then sprinkle with parsley.

Chicken Breast with Vegetables

Ingredients

5.0 oz (142 g) Chicken breast

1.5 oz (43 g) Broccoli

1.5 oz (43 g) Cauliflower

0.5 oz (14 g) Carrot

0.5 oz (14 g) Butter

1/4 teaspoon Oregano

Salt, pepper, and spices to taste

Energy: 290 kcal

Protein: 34 g

Fat: 14 g

Net Carbs: 4 g

Total Carbs: 6 g

Directions

Preheat oven to 360 °F (180 °C). Lightly grease a casserole with cooking oil.

Cut chicken, broccoli, cauliflower, and carrot into chunks; place in the casserole, then mix with oregano and melted butter.

Bake it for ~20 min covered or stirring occasionally.

Sour Chicken Breast with Vegetables

Ingredients

5.0 oz (142 g) Chicken breast

1.5 oz (43 g) Broccoli

1.5 oz (43 g) Cabbage

0.5 oz (14 g) Onion

1.5 oz (43 g) Sour cream

1.0 oz (28 g) Cheese

Salt, pepper, and spices to taste

Energy: 383 kcal

Protein: 41 g

Fat: 20 g

Net Carbs: 6 g

Total Carbs: 8 g

Directions

Preheat oven to 360 °F (180 °C). Lightly grease a casserole with cooking oil.

Cut chicken, broccoli, cabbage, and onion into chunks; place in the casserole, then mix with sour cream.

Bake it for ~20 min covered or stirring occasionally, then place shredded cheese on top. Bake it for extra ~10 min.

Mushroom Chicken Breast

Ingredients

5.0 oz (142 g) Chicken breast

0.5 oz (14 g) Onion

3.5 oz (99 g) Mushroom

1.5 oz (43 g) Cream cheese

1.5 oz (43 g) Cheese

Salt, pepper, and spices to taste

Energy: 493 kcal

Protein: 47 g

Fat: 31 g

Net Carbs: 5 g

Total Carbs: 6 g

Directions

Preheat oven to 360 °F (180 °C). Lightly grease a casserole with cooking oil.

Cut chicken, mushroom, and onion into chunks; place in the casserole, then mix with cream cheese and shredded cheese.

Bake it for ~20 min.

Zucchini Chicken Casserole

Ingredients

5.0 oz (142 g) Chicken breast

5.0 oz (142 g) Zucchini

1.5 oz (43 g) Cheese

0.5 oz (14 g) Mayonnaise (80%)

Salt, pepper, and spices to taste

Energy: 453 kcal

Protein: 44 g

Fat: 28 g

Net Carbs: 4 g

Total Carbs: 5 g

Directions

Preheat oven to 360 °F (180 °C). Lightly grease a casserole with cooking oil.

Cut chicken and zucchini into chunks; place in the casserole, then mix with mayonnaise.

Bake it for ~20 min covered or stirring occasionally, then place shredded cheese on top. Bake it for extra ~10 min.

Four Cheese Chicken Casserole

Ingredients

5.0 oz (142 g) Chicken breast

2.0 oz (57 g) Cheese (mix your favorites, e.g., mozzarella, parmesan, cheddar, gouda)

0.5 oz (14 g) Butter

1 clove garlic

Salt, pepper, and spices to taste

Energy: 463 kcal

Protein: 46 g

Fat: 30 g

Net Carbs: 2 g

Total Carbs: 2 g

Directions

Preheat oven to 360 °F (180 °C). Lightly grease a casserole with cooking oil.

Cut chicken into slices; place in the casserole, mix with melted butter and season with garlic. Place shredded cheese on top.

Bake it for ~20 min.

Sour Chicken Drumsticks

Ingredients

7.0 oz (199 g) Chicken drumsticks

3.5 oz (99 g) Mushroom

1.5 oz (43 g) Sour cream

0.5 oz (14 g) Mustard

Salt, pepper, and spices to taste

Energy: 354 kcal

Protein: 43 g

Fat: 17 g

Net Carbs: 5 g

Total Carbs: 6 g

Directions

Preheat oven to 360 °F (180 °C). Lightly grease a casserole with cooking oil.

Place ingredients in the casserole, mix them.

Bake it for ~45 min turning drumsticks over occasionally or covered.

Tomato Chicken Drumsticks

Ingredients

7.0 oz (199 g) Chicken drumsticks

1.0 oz (28 g) Bell pepper

1.0 oz (28 g) Olive

3.5 oz (99 g) Tomato

1.0 oz (28 g) Tomato sauce

Salt, pepper, and spices to taste

Energy: 308 kcal

Protein: 41 g

Fat: 12 g

Net Carbs: 5 g

Total Carbs: 8 g

Directions

Preheat oven to 360 °F (180 °C). Lightly grease a casserole with cooking oil.

Place ingredients in the casserole, mix them.

Bake it for ~45 min turning drumsticks over occasionally or covered.

Chicken Breast Casserole with Pickles and Bacon

Ingredients

4.2 oz (120 g) Chicken breast

1.5 oz (43 g) Bacon

3.5 oz (99 g) Pickles

1.5 oz (43 g) Sour cream

1.0 oz (28 g) Cheese

Salt, pepper, and spices to taste

Energy: 497 kcal

Protein: 41 g

Fat: 35 g

Net Carbs: 3 g

Total Carbs: 4 g

Directions

Preheat oven to 360 °F (180 °C). Lightly grease a casserole with cooking oil.

Cut chicken, bacon, and pickles into chunks; place in the casserole, then mix with sour cream.

Bake it for ~20 min covered or stirring occasionally, then place shredded cheese on top. Bake it for extra ~10 min.

Eggplant Chicken Breast Casserole

Ingredients

5.0 oz (142 g) Chicken breast

2.0 oz (57 g) Eggplant

2.0 oz (57 g) Tomato

1.5 oz (43 g) Sour cream

1.0 oz (28 g) Cheese

Salt, pepper, and spices to taste

Energy: 375 kcal

Protein: 41 g

Fat: 20 g

Net Carbs: 5 g

Total Carbs: 7 g

Directions

Preheat oven to 360 °F (180 °C). Lightly grease a casserole with cooking oil.

Cut chicken, eggplant, and tomato into slices; place ingredients in the casserole (one layer chicken breast, one layer sour cream, one layer tomato, one layer eggplant).

Bake it for ~20 min, then place shredded cheese on top. Bake it for extra ~10 min.

Spinach Chicken Breast Casserole

Ingredients

5.0 oz (142 g) Chicken breast

3.5 oz (99 g) Spinach

3.5 oz (99 g) Tomato

2 Eggs

Salt, pepper, and spices to taste

Energy: 347 kcal

Protein: 48 g

Fat: 13 g

Net Carbs: 4 g

Total Carbs: 8 g

Directions

Preheat oven to 360 °F (180 °C). Lightly grease a casserole with cooking oil.

Cut chicken, spinach, and tomato into chunks; place in the casserole, then put eggs on top. Season it with your favorite spices.

Bake it for ~20 min.

Cottage Pie

Ingredients

5.0 oz (142 g) Ground beef

1.0 oz (28 g) Ketchup (reduced sugar)

2.0 oz (57 g) Tomato

1.5 oz (43 g) Cream cheese

1.0 oz (28 g) Cheese

Salt, pepper, and spices to taste

Energy: 485 kcal

Protein: 41 g

Fat: 33 g

Net Carbs: 5 g

Total Carbs: 6 g

Directions

Preheat oven to 360 °F (180 °C). Lightly grease a casserole with cooking oil.

Mix ground beef, ketchup, sliced tomato, and salt in the casserole.

Bake it for ~20 min covered or stirring occasionally, then place cream cheese and shredded cheese on top. Bake it for extra ~10 min.

Mushroom Beef Tenderloin

Ingredients

5.0 oz (142 g) Beef tenderloin

2.0 oz (57 g) Demi-Glace sauce (Wegmans)

3.5 oz (99 g) Mushroom

Salt, pepper, and spices to taste

Energy: 269 kcal

Protein: 35 g

Fat: 12 g

Net Carbs: 6 g

Total Carbs: 7 g

Directions

Preheat oven to 360 °F (180 °C). Lightly grease a casserole with cooking oil.

Mix beef tenderloin, demi-glace, and mushroom in the casserole.

Bake it for ~30 min covered or stirring occasionally.

Beef Casserole with Eggplant and Tomato

Ingredients

5.0 oz (142 g) Ground beef

2.0 oz (57 g) Tomato

1.0 oz (28 g) Tomato sauce

2.0 oz (57 g) Eggplant

1.0 oz (28 g) Parmesan

1/8 teaspoon Pepper

Salt, pepper, and spices to taste

Energy: 349 kcal

Protein: 40 g

Fat: 18 g

Net Carbs: 5 g

Total Carbs: 8 g

Directions

Preheat oven to 360 °F (180 °C). Lightly grease a casserole with cooking oil.

Mix ground beef, tomato sauce, and pepper in the casserole.

Bake it for ~20 min covered or stirring occasionally, then arrange sliced eggplant, tomato, and parmesan on top. Bake it for extra ~10 min.

Cabbage Beef Casserole

Ingredients

5.0 oz (142 g) Ground beef

2.0 oz (57 g) Sour cream

2.0 oz (57 g) Tomato

2.0 oz (57 g) Cabbage

1.0 oz (28 g) Cheese

Salt, pepper, and spices to taste

Energy: 452 kcal

Protein: 41 g

Fat: 29 g

Net Carbs: 5 g

Total Carbs: 7 g

Directions

Preheat oven to 360 °F (180 °C). Lightly grease a casserole with cooking oil.

Mix ground beef, sour cream, sliced tomato, and cabbage in the casserole.

Bake it for ~20 min covered or stirring occasionally, then place shredded cheese on top. Bake it for extra ~10 min.

Keto Beef Meatballs

Ingredients

5.0 oz (142 g) Ground beef

1 egg

3.5 oz (99 g) Bell pepper

1.5 oz (43 g) Cheese

Salt, pepper, and spices to taste

Energy: 459 kcal

Protein: 48 g

Fat: 26 g

Net Carbs: 5 g

Total Carbs: 7 g

Directions

Preheat oven to 360 °F (180 °C). Lightly grease a casserole with cooking oil.

Mix ground beef with egg and some salt, make balls and place them in the casserole.

Bake it for ~20 min turning balls over occasionally or covered, then add bell pepper and shredded cheese. Bake it for extra ~10 min.

Beef Casserole with Vegetables

Ingredients

5.0 oz (142 g) Ground beef

0.5 oz (14 g) Butter

1.5 oz (43 g) Tomato

1.5 oz (43 g) Broccoli

0.5 oz (14 g) Onion

0.5 oz (14 g) Pea

Salt, pepper, and spices to taste

Energy: 347 kcal

Protein: 34 g

Fat: 20 g

Net Carbs: 5 g

Total Carbs: 8 g

Directions

Preheat oven to 360 °F (180 °C). Lightly grease a casserole with cooking oil.

Mix ground beef with melted butter, tomato, broccoli, onion, and pea in the casserole.

Bake it for ~30 min covered or stirring occasionally.

Beef Casserole with Egg

Ingredients

5.0 oz (142 g) Ground beef

0.5 oz (14 g) Mustard

2 eggs

Salt, pepper, and spices to taste

Energy: 374 kcal

Protein: 44 g

Fat: 20 g

Net Carbs: 2 g

Total Carbs: 2 g

Directions

Preheat oven to 360 °F (180 °C). Lightly grease a casserole with cooking oil.

Mix ground beef with mustard in the casserole.

Bake it for ~20 min covered or stirring occasionally, then place eggs on top. Bake it for extra ~10 min.

Zucchini Beef Casserole

Ingredients

5.0 oz (142 g) Ground beef

5.3 oz (150 g) Zucchini

0.5 oz (14 g) Mayonnaise (80%)

1.0 oz (28 g) Cheese

Salt, pepper, and spices to taste

Energy: 452 kcal

Protein: 40 g

Fat: 30 g

Net Carbs: 4 g

Total Carbs: 5 g

Directions

Preheat oven to 360 °F (180 °C). Lightly grease a casserole with cooking oil.

Place ground beef, zucchini, and mayonnaise in the casserole.

Bake it for ~20 min covered or stirring occasionally, then place shredded cheese on top. Bake it for extra ~10 min.

Mushroom Beef Casserole

Ingredients

5.0 oz (142 g) Ground beef

3.5 oz (99 g) Mushroom

3.5 oz (99 g) Sour cream

Salt, pepper, and spices to taste

Energy: 431 kcal

Protein: 36 g

Fat: 30 g

Net Carbs: 5 g

Total Carbs: 6 g

Directions

Preheat oven to 360 °F (180 °C). Lightly grease a casserole with cooking oil.

Mix ground beef, mushroom, and sour cream in the casserole.

Bake it for ~30 min covered or stirring occasionally.

Tomato Beef Meatballs

Ingredients

5.0 oz (142 g) Ground beef

1 egg

1.5 oz (43 g) Tomato

0.5 oz (14 g) Onion

1.5 oz (43 g) Tomato sauce

1.0 oz (28 g) Sour cream

1/4 teaspoon Oregano

Salt, pepper, and spices to taste

Energy: 358 kcal

Protein: 38 g

Fat: 20 g

Net Carbs: 5 g

Total Carbs: 7 g

Directions

Preheat oven to 360 °F (180 °C). Lightly grease a casserole with cooking oil.

Mix ground beef, egg, oregano, smashed tomato, and onion. Form balls, place them in the casserole and put tomato sauce on top.

Bake it for ~30 min turning balls over occasionally or covered, then put sour cream on top of the balls.

Mushroom Pork Casserole

Ingredients

5.0 oz (142 g) Pork chop

3.5 oz (99 g) Mushroom

1.5 oz (43 g) Bell pepper

1.5 oz (43 g) Sour cream

1.0 oz (28 g) Cheese

Salt, pepper, and spices to taste

Energy: 403 kcal

Protein: 40 g

Fat: 25 g

Net Carbs: 5 g

Total Carbs: 7 g

Directions

Preheat oven to 360 °F (180 °C). Lightly grease a casserole with cooking oil.

Cut pork, mushroom, and bell pepper into chunks; place in the casserole, then mix with sour cream.

Bake it for ~30 min covered or stirring occasionally, then place shredded cheese on top. Bake it for extra ~10 min.

Cheese Pork Meatballs

Ingredients

5.0 oz (142 g) Ground pork

1.5 oz (43 g) Cream cheese

1.5 oz (43 g) Cheese

Salt, pepper, and spices to taste

Energy: 487 kcal

Protein: 43 g

Fat: 35 g

Net Carbs: 2 g

Total Carbs: 2 g

Directions

Preheat oven to 360 °F (180 °C). Lightly grease a casserole with cooking oil.

Mix ground pork with cream cheese and spices. Form balls and place them in the casserole.

Bake it for ~20 min turning balls over occasionally or covered, then place shredded cheese on top. Bake it for extra ~10 min.

Mustard Pork Casserole

Ingredients

5.0 oz (142 g) Pork chop

0.5 oz (14 g) Mustard

3.5 oz (99 g) Tomato

0.5 oz (14 g) Chives

1.5 oz (43 g) Cheese

Salt, pepper, and spices to taste

Energy: 377 kcal

Protein: 42 g

Fat: 21 g

Net Carbs: 5 g

Total Carbs: 6 g

Directions

Preheat oven to 360 °F (180 °C). Lightly grease a casserole with cooking oil.

Cut pork and tomato into chunks; place in the casserole, then mix with mustard.

Bake it for ~30 min covered or stirring occasionally, then place shredded cheese and chives on top. Bake it for extra ~10 min.

Tomato Pork Casserole

Ingredients

5.0 oz (142 g) Pork chop

1.5 oz (43 g) Tomato sauce

3.5 oz (99 g) Tomato

1.5 oz (43 g) Cheese

Salt, pepper, and spices to taste

Energy: 367 kcal

Protein: 42 g

Fat: 20 g

Net Carbs: 5 g

Total Carbs: 7 g

Directions

Preheat oven to 360 °F (180 °C). Lightly grease a casserole with cooking oil.

Cut pork and tomato into chunks; place in the casserole, then mix with tomato sauce.

Bake it for ~30 min covered or stirring occasionally, then place shredded cheese on top. Bake it for extra ~10 min.

Eggplant Pork Casserole

Ingredients

5.0 oz (142 g) Ground pork

3.5 oz (99 g) Eggplant

1.5 oz (43 g) Cheese

Salt, pepper, and spices to taste

Energy: 366 kcal

Protein: 41 g

Fat: 20 g

Net Carbs: 4 g

Total Carbs: 7 g

Directions

Preheat oven to 360 °F (180 °C). Lightly grease a casserole with cooking oil.

Cut eggplant into thin slices; roll pork into eggplant and place in the casserole.

Bake it for ~30 min turning over occasionally or covered, then place shredded cheese on top. Bake it for extra ~10 min.

Layered Pork Casserole

Ingredients

5.0 oz (142 g) Pork chop

3.5 oz (99 g) Mushroom

3.5 oz (99 g) Tomato

0.5 oz (14 g) Mustard

1.5 oz (43 g) Cheese

Salt, pepper, and spices to taste

Energy: 393 kcal

Protein: 44 g

Fat: 22 g

Net Carbs: 6 g

Total Carbs: 8 g

Directions

Preheat oven to 360 °F (180 °C). Lightly grease a casserole with cooking oil. Add pork chop.

Bake it for ~30 min turning meat over occasionally or covered. Layer mustard, mushroom, tomato, and cheese on top.

Bake it for ~10 min.

Bacon Pork Casserole

Ingredients

4.2 oz (119 g) Pork chop

1.0 oz (28 g) Bacon

3.5 oz (99 g) Broccoli

1.0 oz (28 g) Cream cheese

1.0 oz (28 g) Cheese

Salt, pepper, and spices to taste

Energy: 494 kcal

Protein: 40 g

Fat: 35 g

Net Carbs: 5 g

Total Carbs: 8 g

Directions

Preheat oven to 360 °F (180 °C). Lightly grease a casserole with cooking oil.

Mix chunked pork chop, bacon, broccoli, cream cheese, and cheese in the casserole.

Bake it for ~40 min covered or stirring occasionally.

Bell Pepper Pork Casserole

Ingredients

5.0 oz (142 g) Pork chop

3.5 oz (99 g) Bell pepper

0.5 oz (14 g) Onion

0.5 oz (14 g) Chives

Salt, pepper, and spices to taste

Energy: 227 kcal

Protein: 31 g

Fat: 8 g

Net Carbs: 5 g

Total Carbs: 8 g

Directions

Preheat oven to 360 °F (180 °C). Lightly grease a casserole with cooking oil.

Mix chunked pork chop, bell pepper, onion, and cheese in the casserole.

Bake it for ~30 min covered or stirring occasionally.

Bacon Roast Pork Casserole

Ingredients

5.0 oz (142 g) Pork chop

1.5 oz (43 g) Bacon

1.5 oz (43 g) Onion

Salt, pepper, and spices to taste

Energy: 365 kcal

Protein: 35 g

Fat: 23 g

Net Carbs: 4 g

Total Carbs: 4 g

Directions

Preheat oven to 360 °F (180 °C). Lightly grease a casserole with cooking oil.

Mix pork chop, bacon, and onion in the casserole. Season with your favorite spices

Bake it for ~30 min turning meat over occasionally or covered.

Zucchini Pork Casserole

Ingredients

5.0 oz (142 g) Ground pork

5.3 oz (150 g) Zucchini

1.0 oz (28 g) Cream cheese

1.0 oz (28 g) Cheese

Salt, pepper, and spices to taste

Energy: 412 kcal

Protein: 40 g

Fat: 26 g

Net Carbs: 5 g

Total Carbs: 6 g

Directions

Preheat oven to 360 °F (180 °C). Lightly grease a casserole with cooking oil.

Layer zucchini, ground pork, cream cheese, and cheese in the casserole.

Bake it for ~30 min covered, then uncovered.

Pork Stuffed Cabbage

Ingredients

5.0 oz (142 g) Ground pork

3.5 oz (99 g) Cabbage

1.5 oz (43 g) Sour cream

Salt, pepper, and spices to taste

Energy: 297 kcal

Protein: 32 g

Fat: 16 g

Net Carbs: 5 g

Total Carbs: 7 g

Directions

Preheat oven to 360 °F (180 °C). Lightly grease a casserole with cooking oil.

Mix pork with sour cream and stuff cabbage with this mixture. Place in the casserole.

Bake it for ~30 min turning over occasionally or covered.

Pork Meatballs

Ingredients

5.0 oz (142 g) Ground pork

1 egg

0.5 oz (14 g) Mustard

1.5 oz (43 g) Sour cream

Salt, pepper, and spices to taste

Energy: 357 kcal

Protein: 37 g

Fat: 22 g

Net Carbs: 3 g

Total Carbs: 3 g

Directions

Preheat oven to 360 °F (180 °C). Lightly grease a casserole with cooking oil.

Mix pork with egg and form balls. Place in the casserole.

Bake it for ~25 min turning balls over occasionally or covered, then place mustard-sour cream mixture on top. Bake it for extra 5 min.

Cauliflower Salami Casserole

Ingredients

1.5 oz (43 g) Salami

3.5 oz (99 g) Cauliflower

1.5 oz (43 g) Sour cream

1.5 oz (43 g) Cheese

Salt, pepper, and spices to taste

Energy: 462 kcal

Protein: 23 g

Fat: 39 g

Net Carbs: 5 g

Total Carbs: 7 g

Directions

Preheat oven to 360 °F (180 °C). Lightly grease a casserole with cooking oil.

Mix cauliflower, salami, sour cream, and cheese in the casserole.

Bake it for ~20 min.

Omelet Sausage Casserole

Ingredients

2 eggs

3.5 oz (99 g) Hot dogs

3.5 oz (99 g) Tomato

Salt, pepper, and spices to taste

Energy: 443 kcal

Protein: 25 g

Fat: 36 g

Net Carbs: 4 g

Total Carbs: 5 g

Directions

Preheat oven to 360 °F (180 °C). Lightly grease a casserole with cooking oil.

Mix eggs, chunked hot dogs, and sliced tomato in the casserole.

Bake it for ~20 min.

Green Bean with Bacon

Ingredients

3.5 oz (99 g) Green beans

2.7 oz (77 g) Bacon

1.5 oz (43 g) Cheese

Salt, pepper, and spices to taste

Energy: 464 kcal

Protein: 21 g

Fat: 39 g

Net Carbs: 6 g

Total Carbs: 8 g

Directions

Preheat oven to 360 °F (180 °C). Lightly grease a casserole with cooking oil.

Wrap green beans into bacon and place in the casserole.

Bake it for ~20 min turning over occasionally or covered, then place shredded cheese on top. Bake it for extra ~10 min.

Liver Casserole

Ingredients

5.0 oz (142 g) Liver

0.5 oz (14 g) Mustard

1.5 oz (43 g) Sour cream

Salt, pepper, and spices to taste

Energy: 288 kcal

Protein: 32 g

Fat: 14 g

Net Carbs: 6 g

Total Carbs: 6 g

Directions

Preheat oven to 360 °F (180 °C). Lightly grease a casserole with cooking oil.

Mix liver with mustard and sour cream.

Bake it for ~20 min.

Kingklip Casserole

Ingredients

5.0 oz (142 g) Kingklip fish

0.5 oz (14 g) Onion

3.5 oz (99 g) Tomato

1.5 oz (43 g) Parmesan

Salt, pepper, and spices to taste

Energy: 273 kcal

Protein: 36 g

Fat: 12 g

Net Carbs: 4 g

Total Carbs: 5 g

Directions

Preheat oven to 360 °F (180 °C). Lightly grease a casserole with cooking oil.

Place fish, tomato, and onion in the casserole.

Bake it for ~20 min, then place parmesan on top. Bake it for extra 5 min.

Salmon Casserole

Ingredients

5.0 oz (142 g) Salmon

2.0 oz (57 g) Cream cheese

Salt, pepper, and spices to taste

Energy: 380 kcal

Protein: 35 g

Fat: 26 g

Net Carbs: 2 g

Total Carbs: 2 g

Directions

Preheat oven to 360 °F (180 °C). Lightly grease a casserole with cooking oil.

Place fish in the casserole. Mix cream cheese with water and spices until desired consistency.

Bake it for ~20 min, then pour cream cheese on top. Bake it for extra 5 min.

Broccoli Salmon Casserole

Ingredients

5.0 oz (142 g) Salmon

3.5 oz (99 g) Broccoli

1.5 oz (43 g) Cheese

Salt, pepper, and spices to taste

Energy: 366 kcal

Protein: 45 g

Fat: 19 g

Net Carbs: 5 g

Total Carbs: 7 g

Directions

Preheat oven to 360 °F (180 °C). Lightly grease a casserole with cooking oil.

Mix fish, broccoli, and cheese in the casserole.

Bake it for ~20 min.

Tomato Shrimp Casserole

Ingredients

8.5 oz (241 g) Shrimp

3.5 oz (99 g) Tomato

1.0 oz (28 g) Tomato sauce

Salt, pepper, and spices to taste

Energy: 241 kcal

Protein: 38 g

Fat: 2 g

Net Carbs: 4 g

Total Carbs: 5 g

Directions

Preheat oven to 360 °F (180 °C). Lightly grease a casserole with cooking oil.

Mix shrimp, tomato, and tomato sauce in the casserole.

Bake it for ~20 min.

Butter Shrimp Casserole

Ingredients

8.5 oz (241 g) Shrimp

0.5 oz (14 g) Butter

1/2 teaspoon Herbs de Provence

Salt, pepper, and spices to taste

Energy: 289 kcal

Protein: 36 g

Fat: 11 g

Net Carbs: 3 g

Total Carbs: 3 g

Directions

Preheat oven to 360 °F (180 °C). Lightly grease a casserole with cooking oil.

Mix shrimp, melted butter, and herbs in the casserole.

Bake it for ~20 min.

Mushroom White Fish Casserole

Ingredients

5.0 oz (142 g) Whitefish

3.5 oz (99 g) Mushroom

0.5 oz (14 g) Mayonnaise

1.0 oz (28 g) Cheese

Salt, pepper, and spices to taste

Energy: 470 kcal

Protein: 44 g

Fat: 31 g

Net Carbs: 5 g

Total Carbs: 6 g

Directions

Preheat oven to 360 °F (180 °C). Lightly grease a casserole with cooking oil.

Mix white fish, mushroom, mayonnaise, and cheese in the casserole.

Bake it for ~20 min.

Sour White Fish Casserole

Ingredients

5.0 oz (142 g) Whitefish

0.5 oz (14 g) Onion

1.5 oz (43 g) Sour cream

1.0 oz (28 g) Cheese

Salt, pepper, and spices to taste

Energy: 431 kcal

Protein: 43 g

Fat: 27 g

Net Carbs: 3 g

Total Carbs: 3 g

Directions

Preheat oven to 360 °F (180 °C). Lightly grease a casserole with cooking oil.

Mix white fish, onion, sour cream, and cheese in the casserole.

Bake it for ~20 min.

Mushroom Egg Casserole

Ingredients

3 eggs

3.5 oz (99 g) Mushroom

Salt, pepper, and spices to taste

Energy: 227 kcal

Protein: 21 g

Fat: 14 g

Net Carbs: 5 g

Total Carbs: 6 g

Directions

Preheat oven to 360 °F (180 °C). Lightly grease a casserole with cooking oil.

Mix eggs and mushroom in the casserole.

Bake it for ~15 min.

Sour Zucchini Casserole

Ingredients

5.3 oz (150 g) Zucchini

2.0 oz (57 g) Sour cream

2.0 oz (57 g) Cheese

Salt, pepper, and spices to taste

Energy: 334 kcal

Protein: 17 g

Fat: 28 g

Net Carbs: 5 g

Total Carbs: 6 g

Directions

Preheat oven to 360 °F (180 °C). Lightly grease a casserole with cooking oil.

Mix sliced zucchini, sour cream, and cheese in the casserole.

Bake it for ~20 min.

Brussels Sprouts Casserole

Ingredients

3.5 oz (99 g) Brussels sprouts

3.5 oz (99 g) Cheese

Salt, pepper, and spices to taste

Energy: 392 kcal

Protein: 27 g

Fat: 28 g

Net Carbs: 6 g

Total Carbs: 10 g

Directions

Preheat oven to 360 °F (180 °C). Lightly grease a casserole with cooking oil.

Mix Brussels sprouts and cheese in the casserole.

Bake it for ~20 min.

Cabbage Zucchini Casserole

Ingredients

3.5 oz (99 g) Zucchini

3.5 oz (99 g) Cabbage

0.5 oz (14 g) Mayonnaise

2.0 oz (57 g) Cheese

Salt, pepper, and spices to taste

Energy: 348 kcal

Protein: 16 g

Fat: 28 g

Net Carbs: 6 g

Total Carbs: 9 g

Directions

Preheat oven to 360 °F (180 °C). Lightly grease a casserole with cooking oil.

Mix zucchini, cabbage, mayonnaise, and cheese in the casserole.

Bake it for ~20 min.

Eggplant Zucchini Casserole

Ingredients

3.5 oz (99 g) Zucchini

2.0 oz (57 g) Eggplant

3.5 oz (99 g) Tomato

2.0 oz (57 g) Cheese

Salt, pepper, and spices to taste

Energy: 246 kcal

Protein: 17 g

Fat: 16 g

Net Carbs: 6 g

Total Carbs: 10 g

Directions

Preheat oven to 360 °F (180 °C). Lightly grease a casserole with cooking oil.

Mix zucchini, eggplant, tomato, and cheese in the casserole.

Bake it for ~20 min.

Tomato Eggplant Casserole

Ingredients

3.5 oz (99 g) Tomato

2.0 oz (57 g) Eggplant

1.0 oz (28 g) Tomato sauce

2.0 oz (57 g) Cheese

Salt, pepper, and spices to taste

Energy: 236 kcal

Protein: 16 g

Fat: 16 g

Net Carbs: 6 g

Total Carbs: 9 g

Directions

Preheat oven to 360 °F (180 °C). Lightly grease a casserole with cooking oil.

Mix tomato, eggplant, tomato sauce, and cheese in the casserole.

Bake it for ~20 min.

Egg Kale Casserole

Ingredients

3 eggs

3.5 oz (99 g) Kale

2.0 oz (57 g) Cheese

Salt, pepper, and spices to taste

Energy: 433 kcal

Protein: 34 g

Fat: 30 g

Net Carbs: 4 g

Total Carbs: 7 g

Directions

Preheat oven to 360 °F (180 °C). Lightly grease a casserole with cooking oil.

Mix eggs, kale, and cheese in the casserole.

Bake it for ~20 min.

Tomato Mushroom Casserole

Ingredients

5.0 oz (142 g) Tomato

5.0 oz (142 g) Mushroom

3.5 oz (99 g) Cheese

Salt, pepper, and spices to taste

Energy: 402 kcal

Protein: 29 g

Fat: 29 g

Net Carbs: 4 g

Total Carbs: 5 g

Directions

Preheat oven to 360 °F (180 °C). Lightly grease a casserole with cooking oil.

Mix tomato, mushroom, and cheese in the casserole.

Bake it for ~20 min.

You're Just One Keto Game Away From...

Getting Into The Best Shape Of Your Life

Feeling Confident

Gaining All-day Energy And Focus

Join Us And Be A Keto Player!

https://www.getelan.com/Keto-Game

Made in United States
Troutdale, OR
01/05/2025